A GUIDE TO
QABALISTIC
ASTROLOGY

A GUIDE TO
QABALISTIC
ASTROLOGY

BY

HORUS

SAMUEL WEISER   NEW YORK

Published by
Samuel Weiser, Inc.
740 Broadway
New York City, N.Y. 10003

ISBN 0-87728-368-0

Printed in the
United States of America
by Noble Offset Printers, Inc.
New York City

TABLE OF CONTENTS

PREFACE

This is not a book for beginners. The beginner is advised to start at the beginning with Charles Carter's *The Principles of Astrology*.

This book is for the intermediate or advanced student of Astrology, for herein are lessons suitable to expand and clarify his understanding of the subject. Familiarity with the terms of Astrology, and with the erection and delineation of a Natus, is necessary to a complete comprehension of this book.

Familiarity with the works of Carter, and also Aleister Crowley's *Astrology*, is helpful. If you have not read these works, I would recommend them highly. (The latter book, like this one, is best suited to the intermediate and advanced stages of study.)

Of course, there are other great works on the subject, and Qabalistic texts which can help. I am impressed and pleased with the work and method of the Church of Light, even though I have found that I cannot agree with all of their findings.

No proof is offered herein as to the validity of Astrology. It is assumed that the reader has already satisfied his intellect in this regard, and knows there are numerous books already dealing with the subject, making any discussion of it superfluous. There is no method for erecting the chart herein, no delineations of aspects, no significances of the planets in the twelve signs, etc.

What I have attempted to do is to heighten the reader's awareness of the implications of his Science, and to resolve matters where heretofore in Astrology there has existed uncertainty and contradiction. I have emphasized the link between Astrology and the Qabalah. I have added a contribution to the literature of Pluto. And finally, I have reconstituted the Astrological Tree of Life, and given the student some of the lesser known but highly important and advanced keys to the Science.

LESSON 1

A Book The Student Must Read

The first work of the student is to obtain and study *The Qabalah of Aleister Crowley* (published by Samuel Weiser, Inc.).*

Several of the discourses I am presenting herein necessitate the understanding of Astrology as a Qabalistic Science, and no other distillation of the Qabalah will suit this purpose nearly as well.

The earnest student need not be discouraged if upon opening my book it is immediately found that another book will be needed. This work of Crowley's shall abundantly reward study. The Introduction and Book Three may be dispensed with altogether (i.e., for these purposes). Book One, entitled Gematria, must be borne, as it lays down the foundation for a fuller comprehension of Book Two. (These Books, incidentally, are all contained in one volume).

One need not read the books Crowley recommends at the beginning of Gematria. (Again, I say this only in reference to our Astrological purposes). It is unlikely that the student will immediately comprehend everything presented, however. Patience may be required. Gloss over nothing. Thus will everything that is germane to this work be understood.

By the time the reader has finished Book Two (*Liber 777*),† Astrology shall appear to the student, as it should, as a Qabalistic Science. This mode of perception will be the key to the fullest comprehension of those essays in this book which deal with Astrology in this Light, and hopefully much more than that.‡

---

*If the student has already made an earnest study of the Qabalah, is familiar with the Tree of Life, and knows something of the numerological and astrological modes as regards Magickal tables of correspondence, Lesson 1 may be dispensed with.

†The reader need not venture beyond page 137 of this Book. (Total reading requested: 210 pages).

‡Upon beginning this study, the student may find himself wondering how the subject matter is related to Astrology. However, if the study is completed, the relationship and the implications will become apparent to the reader. The reader is also encouraged to read the unrequested portions of "The Qabalah of Aleister Crowley" (S. Weiser), if he is inclined to do so.

LESSON 2

The Qabalistic System Of Astrological Planetary
Rulerships, Octaves, Exaltations, Etc.

Ever since the discovery of Uranus, Neptune and Pluto, there has existed some confusion and uncertainty as to the rulerships and exaltations of these planets. The essential truths have appeared in the light of further research, however, and these are the relating of Uranus with Aquarius, Neptune with Pisces, and Pluto with Scorpio.

However, based on work which was begun by Charles Carter, and in the light of the Qabalistic key of Correspondences, it is our firm belief that the chart on page five shows the perfection of the planetary rulerships of the signs. (See CHART I.)

Starting with the Lights and their signs, we take first what may be called the Solar Rulership System. This begins with Leo. Note that as you move forward (through Virgo, Libra, Scorpio, etc.), the planets ruling the signs fall in order of closeness to the Sun.

The Solar Rulership System ends at the top of the third column (SECONDARY RULER), where Pluto is listed as the secondary ruler of Aries, which is its positive-regenerative mode, and which makes a fitting point for the end of this system, as it is the exaltation of Sol.

The second or Lunar Rulership System begins with Cancer and moves backwards. Once again the planets fall in order of closeness to the Sun. As we continue around the zodiac, and backwards beyond Aries, the secondary rulers complete the system, starting upwards from the bottom of the third column with Jupiter, and ending with Pluto as the secondary ruler (also) of Scorpio, House of Death. Thus we have a fitting ending point for the Lunar Rulership System, as Scorpio is the detriment of Luna.

Note that all planets have double rulerships, with one positive expression and one negative.

CHART I

PLANETARY RULERSHIPS

SIGN	RULER	SECONDARY RULER
ARIES	MARS	PLUTO
TAURUS	VENUS	
GEMINI	MERCURY	
CANCER	MOON	
LEO	SUN	
VIRGO	MERCURY	
LIBRA	VENUS	
SCORPIO	MARS	PLUTO
SAGITTARIUS	JUPITER	NEPTUNE
CAPRICORN	SATURN	URANUS
AQUARIUS	URANUS	SATURN
PISCES	NEPTUNE	JUPITER

Charles Carter has explored the relationship between Saturn and Uranus, as well as the relationship between Jupiter and Neptune, in his book, *The Zodiac and the Soul*.

The Church of Light gave expression to the latter relationship when it claimed Neptune's exaltation to be Sagittarius. (This is an error, but an error easy to understand).

The Qabalistic perfection of this system of rulership, i.e., its perfect order, cannot be denied.

Let us now note that the rulership systems have not brought us all the way around back to the Lights.

Furthermore, Pluto has been given secondary rulerships only, and is unique in this respect. This suggests the Octave.

Picking up where we left off, we find the perfect order continuing with the System of Octaves.

CHART II

THE SYSTEM OF OCTAVES

THE SOLAR SYSTEM

ARIES-PLUTO: Mars rules Aries. Pluto is the octave of Mars.

TAURUS-NEPTUNE: Venus rules Taurus. Neptune is the octave of Venus.

GEMINI-URANUS: Mercury rules Gemini. Uranus is the octave of Mercury.

THE LUNAR SYSTEM

SCORPIO-PLUTO: Mars rules Scorpio. Pluto is the octave of Mars.

LIBRA-NEPTUNE: Venus rules Libra. Neptune is the octave of Venus.

VIRGO-URANUS: Mercury rules Virgo. Uranus is the octave of Mercury.

Note how both the Solar and Lunar Systems of Rulerships and Octaves end at the gate of the sign of its opposite pole. (Furthermore, the planets are proceeding in the same order, only we are progressing in the opposite direction, from Pluto, the planet most distant from the Sun. Finally, coming to the sign of the opposite pole suggests the next system to follow in the flow of Qabalistic order, that of Detriments.)

CHART III

THE SYSTEM OF DETRIMENTS

THE SOLAR SYSTEM	THE LUNAR SYSTEM
LEO-URANUS	CANCER-URANUS
CANCER-SATURN	LEO-SATURN
GEMINI-JUPITER (AND NEPTUNE)	VIRGO-JUPITER (AND NEPTUNE)
TAURUS-MARS (AND PLUTO)	LIBRA-MARS (AND PLUTO)
ARIES-VENUS	SCORPIO-VENUS
PISCES-MERCURY	SAGITTARIUS-MERCURY
AQUARIUS-THE SUN	CAPRICORN-THE MOON

Of course, the student should already know that the detriment of a planet is the sign opposite the sign it rules. In this system, each planet has two detriments. The Lights are exceptions, but then this is logical since they also rule only one sign each.

We have arrived now at the System of Exaltations (CHART IV). As with the System of Detriments, the principle of opposite signs is involved, but it is further compounded by polarizations between the celestial bodies, inherent in the previous system. Thus Sol, whose detriment is in the Saturnian sign, Aquarius, is exalted in Aries, the sign opposite Saturn's exaltation, Libra. (As to why the Sun should be exalted in Aries to begin with, the student is advised to seek the answer in Ptolemy's *Tetrabiblios*, if he does not know it. The Moon's exaltation is also explained therein.)

CHART IV

THE SYSTEM OF EXALTATIONS

SUN IN ARIES   SATURN IN LIBRA

MOON IN TAURUS   URANUS IN SCORPIO

(N. NODE IN GEMINI)   (S. NODE IN SAGITTARIUS)

JUPITER IN CANCER   MARS IN CAPRICORN

PLUTO IN LEO   NEPTUNE IN AQUARIUS

MERCURY IN VIRGO   VENUS IN PISCES

The Moon, whose detriment is in the Uranian sign, Capricorn, is exalted in Taurus, the sign opposite Uranus' exaltation, Scorpio.

The polarity of the Nodes will certainly not be questioned. Thus their exaltations form another key to this method of determining exaltations.

The polarity of Jupiter and Mars is indirect, but derives from the fact that these planets have been related in the rulership systems to Neptune and Pluto, respectively. These planets, in turn, are the octaves of opposites, Venus and Mars. This also explains the next pair of exaltations.

In the last pair of exaltations, Venus, for her part, reflects her octave Neptune, whose signs are the detriment of Mercury.

In the last pair of exaltations, Venus, for her part, reflects her octave Neptune, whose signs are the detriment of Mercury.

I should like to add further notes on four of these assignations:

§ § §

1. MERCURY IN VIRGO: This is the classical exaltation of Mercury, affirmed in the majority of astrological works. However, the Church of Light has named Aquarius the exaltation of Mercury. While it is easy to see how this was derived, they are, nevertheless, in error.

2. URANUS IN SCORPIO: This is also confirmed by Raphael and Crowley. Once again, I make special note of this because the Church of Light has designated Gemini to be the exaltation of Uranus. Again, this is understandable, but inaccurate.

3. NEPTUNE IN AQUARIUS: We have previously discussed the error made by the Church of Light as regards the exaltation of Neptune. Crowley made the accurate assignation in his *The Book of Thoth*. (Yet he also made the gross error of making Leo the exaltation of Uranus in this book. All the same, as implied in the previous note, Crowley rectified this in his "Astrology", although it appears he became reluctant to assign any exaltation to Neptune at all.)

Thus the student may find the precedents weak, and justly ask why Aquarius should be the exaltation of Neptune.

Uranus rules Aquarius, which it represents. On the Tree of Life, which will be discussed in Lesson 4, Uranus corresponds with Wisdom, the Magickal Path, the second sephira (principle or number) and Neptune corresponds to the third, Understanding, the Mystical Path. The exaltation of Neptune in Aquarius suggests Understanding (passive) becoming Wisdom (active). Consider that, similarly, Uranus is exalted in Scorpio which represents, in our present system, Pluto as Kether, the Crown, the first of the Sephiroth.

4. PLUTO IN LEO: (See LESSON 5: PLUTO). All I should like to say now in this regard is that the Church of Light and I are in full agreement on this point, and that their determination of Pluto's exaltation preceded mine, and was most helpful to me in developing the Qabalistic System of Exaltations.

§ § §

Let the student now note the Fall of each planet, the sign opposite its exaltation, and Lesson 2 is concluded.

LESSON 3

The Lights: An Exercise In The Qabalistic Method Of Determining Astrological Correspondences

Perhaps the simplicity of the Qabalists's approach to astrology can best be shown by demonstrating some of the significances of the Sun and the Moon, beginning with the most commonplace observations, and then tracing out the implications to a limited point. This point must be limited, for otherwise the significances will merge into the infinite and overlap, thus creating chaos when the object is to divine the order.

As the object is simply to make commonplace observations (and to derive further correspondences from these), it should be apparent that the Qabalistic method requires only patience, concentration, and imagination.

Let us make note that it was the Qabalistic method which enabled Marc Edmund Jones to realize and introduce his *"Guide to Horoscope Interpretation."*

Research, in particular, the evaluation of numerous charts, of course, was a necessary aid, and the student is advised to incorporate research into his Qabalistic method. Furthermore, he should improve upon his ability to make Qabalistic connections by studying the science of Astronomy, Roman and Greek Mythology, and the Thoth Tarot.

We begin with the Sun, then. It is not necessary to be an astrologer to relate the following correspondences to the Sun: Light, the Day, Fire, Heat, Centrality, Energy, Power, and Life itself, for example. We could not live without the Sun.

The next step, then, would be to trace out the implications of those just named commonplace observations.

9

§ § §

LIGHT: We might start by associating the Light with God, which is technically correct, although we are thus at once lost in the infinite, as all things are God.

Again, we might, recalling the words, "I am the Light of the World," associate the Solar principle with the Lord Jesus Christ, God in focused manifestation as the Son. We may assume also that the Sun represents Christ, or "the spark of God" within each of us (life itself again), our true nature and individuality. As Christ is the Son of God, we also have our first suggestion that the Sun rules sons, i.e., the male sex. It is the polarity which is called Yang in the I Ching, positive and strong.

LIFE: Let us add, then, vitality and health, vigor and Spirit, for example.

POWER AND CENTRALITY: Positions of authority, command and leadership, etc.

HEAT AND FIRE: The qualities of warmth and intense ardor, etc.

THE DAY: As opposed to night, when we retire, the day is a time when we are outgoing.

ENERGY: Self-expression.

§ § §

More could be derived from these observations, and we could add astronomical and mythological implications as well. However, the point is only to instruct the student in the method.

The polarities between the celestial bodies can provide clues, also. Let us take a brief look at the Moon.

Instantly, we can associate Night with the Moon. Since day and night are opposites, we can assume that the Moon is the complementary pole of the Sun.

Thus, instead of self-expression, we judge receptivity; instead of the masculine principle, we judge the feminine principle; instead of fire, we judge water, etc.

However, we must not assume that the Moon rules death. It is one of the Lights, and as it is the feminine principle, it is nourishing, motherly, protective, etc.

The student is advised to use this method to expand his know-ledge of astrological correspondences beyond that which can be obtained in books, although he is advised to use the works of at least several reliable authors to check whether or not he is on the right track.

CHART V

VII English of Col. VI.	III. English of Col. II.	I. Key Scale.
. . . .	Nothing . . . . No Limit . . . . Limitless L.V.X. .	0
Sphere of the Primum Mobile	Crown	1
Sphere of the Zodiac or Fixed Stars . .	Wisdom	2
Sphere of Saturn	Understanding . . .	3
Sphere of Jupiter	Mercy	4
Sphere of Mars	Strength	5
Sphere of Sol	Beauty	6
Sphere of Venus	Victory	7
Sphere of Mercury	Splendour	8
Sphere of Luna	Foundation	9
Sphere of the Elements	Kingdom	10

LESSON 4

A Reconstitution Of The Astrological Tree Of Life

The reader is asked to note Chart V, a reproduction of pages 2 and 3 of "The Qabalah of Aleister Crowley," Liber 777, the Table of Correspondences. Observe the Sephiroth in Column III, and also the Astrological correspondences in Column VII (Key Scale: numbers 1-10).

In Crowley's *The Book of Thoth* (S. Weiser paperback), he states, "The astronomical discoveries of Herschel (Uranus), Neptune, and Pluto have completed the tenfold scheme of the Sephiroth. . ."

While the published Qabalah of Crowley contains no correspondences for Pluto (because the planet had not yet been discovered), this later *Book of Thoth* tackled the problem keeping the positions of the Earth and the Septenary (the seven planets, Sephiroth nine through three) intact, and attributing Pluto, Neptune and Uranus to the Crown, Wisdom, and the Abyss, respectively. Chart V does not show the Abyss, because it is not a true Sephira, but its position is indicated in Chart VII.

However, while Crowley's rectification in "Thoth" is, undeniably, magickal and qabalistic perfection, it is not really a tenfold scheme, but an elevenfold scheme. It is perfect, nevertheless, because the celestial bodies are numbered in the actual order in which they are found in the Solar System, i.e., with easily explained exceptions. The Sun's position is reversed with those of the Earth and Moon (which belong together), just as the Earth is, for us, the true starting point, while the Sun is the true center of the Solar System, after all. Furthermore, although Uranus seems to be out of place (when listed numerically, the unnumbered Abyss falls between Jupiter and Saturn), when the Tree of Life is drawn diagrammatically the Abyss falls, in a (limited) sense, between Saturn and Neptune.

However, although this system has its perfection and keeps with tradition, purely astrological considerations can leave one dissatisfied. For example, Crowley's earlier ascription of the Asteroids to the disintegrative Abyss has a greater ring of truth than the consideration of a planet, Uranus, here as a non-Sephira.

The reader might find himself justifiably exasperated by the confusion of the diversified systems. We have not yet even mentioned the fact that if one tries to replace the *Liber 777* planetary attributions with those given in *"The Book of Thoth,"* although the septenary remains intact, he will wind up with such situations as the God Uranus being ascribed to the planet Neptune, which is obviously incorrect.

The rectification in "Thoth" is a perfect Qabalistic picture of the Solar System.

It is not the author's purpose herein to revise the entire Tables of Magickal Correspondences (Liber 777). This is an astrological treatise. Those using the tables in 777 are advised to assign Pluto to Zero, with which, as representative of death and for other reasons, it bears a kinship. The Tables and appendages in 777 are the work of tremendous scholarship, and are part of the most sublime Magickal system in existence. Thus, it is my understatement if I say that this system is not without its virtue.

Yet, herein, determined by astrological considerations, is the author's personal system. Only the planetary assignations have been altered, and this is all that is meant by "the Astrological Tree of Life," and the reconstitution thereof, so that this Astrological Tree of Life has been reconstituted primarily as an aid, a Qabalistic key, for the astrologer and the student of Astrology.

However, if we can see the obvious relationship between Astrology and the Qabalah, we should agree that one must fit most adeptly and neatly into the other, otherwise Astrology loses its connection with the Tree of Life.

After all, is it not written:

> "In the midst of the street of it, and on either side
> of the river, was there the tree of life, which bare
> twelve manner of fruits, and yielded her fruit every
> month: and the leaves of the tree were for the
> healing of the nations."
>
> (Rev. 22:2)

(See CHART VI.)

(Note: It has hardly been my intention to belittle the work of Aleister Crowley, whose contribution to the world of Uranian literature* stands unsurpassed).

CHART VI

THE RECONSTITUTION OF THE QABALISTIC PLANETARY CORRESPONDENCES

KEY	SEPHIROTH	SPHERE OF
1.	THE CROWN	PLUTO
2.	WISDOM	URANUS
3.	UNDERSTANDING	NEPTUNE
4.	MERCY	JUPITER
5.	SEVERITY (STRENGTH)	SATURN
6.	BEAUTY	THE SUN
7.	VICTORY	VENUS
8.	SPLENDOR	MERCURY
9.	THE FOUNDATION	MARS
10.	THE KINGDOM	THE MOON

*Magick, the Qabalah, the Tarot, Astrology, etc.

EXPLANATIONS

(from the lowest to the highest principles)

10. MALKUTH, THE EARTH, THE KINGDOM: ATTRIBU-
TION: THE MOON.

The Kingdom is the Earth, of course, the realm of Matter, and of the four elements fire, water, air and earth itself. But, astrologically, the earth is a body which is acted upon but does not act and consequently, the ten celestial bodies astrological which are to correspond to the ten Sephiroth do not include the earth itself, although this is the traditional assignation to Malkuth. Therefore, in consistency with the symbolistic nature of Astrology (and, indeed, of all the Qabalistic Sciences), we take, for Malkuth, a symbol of the earth, the Moon, the light which travels about the earth, describing an imaginary boundary, thus symbolizing the Kingdom. Even the air, the atmosphere, is a part of the Kingdom, and all of this is enclosed within the Moon's circle. Thus it is more noteworthy that Malkuth is also called the Gate, when we consider Luna here.

The Moon rules the water sign Cancer, the sign of the Mother, feminine and receptive. Malkuth is also called the inferior Mother, and the Queen. The Moon's water-nature does reflect a fact of the kingdom, viz., the earth's surface, 70% water.

The Moon's light is but the reflection of the Sun, just as the Kingdom simply signifies the realm of matter which is dependent upon the animation of the Sun, the sustainer of life.

It can be noted, too, that Crowley gave to the Moon the most physical of assessments in *Liber 777*, page 44, in the brief section entitled "The Genethliac Values of the Planets." Here are attributed the Senses and Bodily Consciousness.

§ § §

9. YESOD, THE FOUNDATION: ATTRIBUTION: MARS.

In this system Mars, and not the Moon, is Yesod, the Foundation, and thus it falls below the realm of Mercury (Hod), and therefore of the mind; Mars represents the basic energy of the universe, which differs from that of the Sun in that the Sun, being a

Light, represents a center of conscious direction of energy, and Mars represents brute force. The nature of this fundamental energy is aggressive, and therefore requires constructive channeling and intelligent direction. Otherwise, there is a tendency to discord. Unchecked, Mars does battle.

Wisely employed this energy builds and works for man, not against him. But this is not a higher Sephira, as Tiphereth (the Sun), which is capable of directing it.

Note that Yesod is represented among the angels by Aishim, the Flames. This, by itself, is not as significant as it may seem, considering Mars' fiery nature. What is significant is that these angels are also called the Virile Ones.

In Magickal tradition Mars has been regarded to be more exalted than the Sun, but I should like to point out that this occurs in a seven planet system which never took Uranus, Neptune and Pluto into consideration.

Finally, the Archangel Gabriel is associated with Yesod. He is the angel of the Resurrection (Aries). His trumpet, or horn, is phallic. Both Yesod and Mars are linked with the genitals. The Kingdom (the Moon) is impregnated (with the energy), but Yesod (Mars) impregnates.

§ § §

8. HOD, SPLENDOR: ATTRIBUTION: MERCURY.

Hod has been called Splendor, and also Order. Mercury is the classic attribution, and much discussion is not needed. Mercury is the mind which will direct the energy, brains over brawn as it were. Order is linked with the training of the mind, and Splendor is the realm of learning, education.

The Archangel Raphael is attributed here, and he is both teacher and healer, both faculties of Mercury. It is interesting to note that he is, specifically, the healer of war wounds, another substantiation of this position above Mars.

§ § §

7. NETZACH, VICTORY: ATTRIBUTION: VENUS.

Again, this is the traditional attribution, corroborated by Crowley. What is implied is that true Victory means Peace and

Accord. The ultimate of all this is Love. Netzach is also called Firmness, the quality in Love which is its Victory. Furthermore, Love and Peace temper and firm up the mind, and steer some of the energy of Yesod into the Pillar of Mercy. Firmness also suggests fixed earth, or Taurus, one of the signs of Venus. The Victory expressed here is particularly that of two souls united in Love. (Jupiter is the Higher Love.)

§ § §

6. TIPHERETH, BEAUTY: ATTRIBUTION: THE SUN.
This is, once again, the traditional attribution. The Sun, vital center of the solar system, rules Leo, the sign which governs the heart, and certainly, Tiphereth is the vital center, the heart of the Tree of Life.
Apollo, the Sun God, was called the god of manly beauty.
The Sun is the Light of Life, the spark of God in all human beings.
The progression is such that, given form (Malkuth), energy (Yesod), a mental plane (Hod) and firmness (Netzach), we come to a self, to man, a center of consciousness (which is not the mind itself); we come to a directing force.
Let us note that the Sun represents both Christ and the Beast. The resolution of these two diverse considerations comes when, seeing that the Sun is not the Inscrutable Height (Kether), we find that it is like the innocence of man in Eden. Christ gave us the highest essence of this, purity; the Beast reflected the quality of innocence, albeit in his guiltless, remorseless execution of his work. This reminds us that the higher principles are yet necessary, lest man be no more than a beast. (There is further discussion of the Sun as Beauty in Lesson 7.)

§ § §

5. GEBURAH, SEVERITY: ATTRIBUTION: SATURN.
Here the traditional assignation is Mars, which in the present system we attribute to Yesod, lower on the Tree of Life.
The ideas of Justice, Severity and Karmic Retribution, which belong here, bear greater kinship to Saturn.
The title Strength has also been given to Geburah, and this

does suggest Mars. However, under closer examination, it can be seen that this particular Strength comes from concentration and self-discipline, qualities of Saturn. Certainly, Saturn's exaltation in Libra, sign of the scales of Justice, provides yet another astrological key. Geburah is also called the Power, and the ringed planet does indeed represent a fearsome power. The balance to Chesed (Mercy), called the Giver, should be the Taker. And Time (Saturn) does bear the sickle. Saturn restricts, sets down limitations, and tests.

4. CHESED, MERCY: ATTRIBUTION: JUPITER.

This Sephira is also called Gedulah, Magnificence, or Glory. So now we have the Giver as well as the Taker; as we have seen the Power, now we see the Glory.

Mercy, a higher love, good will, kindness, tolerance and expansiveness all correspond to Jupiter, the Greater Benefic.

This is the traditional attribution.

§ § §

3. BINAH, UNDERSTANDING: ATTRIBUTION: NEPTUNE.

In the seven planet system, Binah has always been assigned Saturn. Binah is Understanding, and is regarded as being passive and feminine.

Neptune rules Pisces; Saturn rules Capricorn. Both are feminine signs.

But Binah is water. The Great Sea is a synonym for Binah. This corresspponds with Pisces and Neptune, who rules the Sea. Binah is also the superior Mother. This is Mary (Mary= Mare=Sea).

Depth is associated with Understanding, and the sea is called the Deep. Darkness is associated with Binah, and the sea is dark, for we cannot see but the surface.

In his "Book 4", Crowley equates Binah with the Magick Cup, which contains bitterness, blood and intoxication.

Intoxication (wine) is Neptunian. The blood is known to consist primarily of sea water. And bitterness? Crowley has called Neptune the "Soul of Tears!"

Also represented is the intuition; the mystic mode, meditation and the mystical states and trances.

§ § §

2. CHOKMAH, WISDOM: ATTRIBUTION: URANUS.

Chokmah is the masculine complement to Binah. It is the Father, and is attributed to the sphere of the Zodiac. No planet better corresponds to this than Uranus, which most astrologers agree governs their science. Uranus governs Aquarius, a masculine sign.

Of course, Chokmah is said to be fire, and Aquarius is an air sign. However, as Crowley said, looking deep into the nature of Uranus, "if we have called Neptune the Soul of the Sea, then Uranus is the essence of Volcanic Fire." He was in accord with this attribution.

Chokmah is also the Logos, the Word, and this corresponds to Uranus as higher octave of Mercury, also called the Logos. Thus Chokmah encompasses the Qabalah, called the Secret Wisdom. Even more important, Chokmah is active, and it represents the Magickal Will, and the path of Magick. It is associated with the wand and the phallus. It is also the rod that becomes the serpent. The serpent is also a symbol of wisdom.

Quoting Crowley:

> "Uranus is the Royal Uraeus Serpent
> in Egyptian Symbolism."

§ § §

1. KETHER, THE CROWN: ATTRIBUTION: PLUTO.

In this system Pluto is the Crown.

Kether is called the Supreme Unity, also the Inscrutable Height. It is the Self of Deity, related to the Most Holy Ancient One, the Creator and Father of all things. The God-name attributed is Eheieh, AHIH, I am. Existence. He is Macroprosopus, and the Father referred to by the Son in Christianity.

He is said to be partly concealed (Scorpio) and partly manifest (Aries).

(The qualities of ultimate power, inscrutability and unity are discussed in the astrological treatment of Pluto in the fifth lesson in this book.)

Let us consider here, however, that Aries is the exaltation of the Sun. One reason for this, not to be found in Ptolemy's Tetrabiblios, is that Aries here reflects Pluto as Kether, and this exaltation represents the direct relationship between the Son and the Father, that the Son (the Sun) is at its best (exaltation) when at one with the Father (Kether-Pluto-Aries).

Also Pluto is exalted in Leo, as the Father is in the Son.

As the last link in the chain of the Solar System, Pluto bears the same unique relationship to the infinite beyond that Kether the Unity bears to Zero, the Limitless.

Kether is called the root of air, and the balance of fire (Aries) and water (Scorpio). The actual coldness of Pluto, which must be a burning coldness, reflects its middle pillar aspect, insofar as the quality of coldness is associated with Indifference. (Indifference is the Buddhist meditation Crowley ascribed to Kether.)

The sexual element of Pluto typifies what is meant by Kether being the very tip of Yod (the Hebrew I) which is the Phallus.

§ § §

CHART VII

DIAGRAM OF THE RECONSTITUTED
ASTROLOGICAL TREE OF LIFE

1
PLUTO
THE CROWN

3
NEPTUNE
UNDERSTANDING

2
URANUS
WISDOM

(Daath)
THE ABYSS

5
SATURN
SEVERITY

4
JUPITER
MERCY

6
THE SUN
BEAUTY

8
MERCURY
SPLENDOR

7
VENUS
VICTORY

9
MARS
THE FOUNDATION

10
THE MOON
THE KINGDOM

CHART VIII

THE THREE PILLARS OF THE TREE OF LIFE

THE MIDDLE PILLAR

PLUTO

THE SUN

MARS

THE MOON

THE PILLAR OF MERCY

URANUS

JUPITER

VENUS

THE PILLAR OF SEVERITY

NEPTUNE

SATURN

MERCURY

LESSON 5

PLUTO

Pluto is the higher octave of Mars. It is called the secondary ruler of both Scorpio and Aries, because it is arrived at secondarily, after Mars. As it is the octave we may assume it governs strongly, on its own plane.

It is not the octave of the Moon as has been supposed by Elbert Benjamine, President of the Church of Light, in his *"The Influence of the Planet Pluto"* (Aries Press). We recommend this book nevertheless, by the way, as there is much valuable information contained in it, despite its brevity. The errors in it stand corrected here, but accurate information will be found in that book which will not be given here.

Nevertheless, returning to the subject of the octave, let us note that Pluto-ruled Scorpio is the fall of the Moon, which makes Pluto an unlikely octave. The Qabalistic perfection of the system of octaves cannot be denied. Furthermore, Pluto is exalted in Leo, which further aligns it to the opposite pole, to the Sun, and fire. Certainly, there are factors in the Scorpionic side of Pluto (water and coldness, for example) which can link it to the Moon. It was also discovered in Cancer, the natural sign of the Moon. What this refers to is the middle pillar of the Tree of Life, where Pluto is linked to the Moon, but less directly than to the Sun and Mars. I should also like to suggest that the Moon is complete in herself, i.e., she has no octave. (Water and coldness are factors also found in the Piscean modes of Jupiter and Neptune.)

Pluto is cold. The life-giving energies of the Sun have to travel an average of approximately 3 billion, 7 hundred million miles to reach Pluto.

This coldness, this distance from the source of light and life, as well as the mythological attributions (Pluto, Hades, etc.), suggests Scorpio, the House of Death.

Pluto's journey around the Sun takes the longest amount of time evidenced by any of the planets. In this way it is again the most lifeless, like the discarnate soul, occult.

This is the first link with Mars. As regards death, Pluto is "abetted" by Mars. But every death is also a birth, which is particularly apparent at the spiritual level, if not so apparent at the physical level. This is the Immortality of God.

Thus, in ruling death, Pluto assimilates as well the rule of physical birth, spiritual death and rebirth.

This rulership of birth and rebirth links Pluto with Mars again as co-ruler of Aries, in its positive mode. It will be noted that Easter, the celebration of the Resurrection of Christ, falls when the Sun is in Aries, exalted. Leo, the sign of the Sun, is the exaltation of Pluto.

As regards the Scorpionic mode of Pluto, once again, it is as if Mars has selfishly pulled the Sun's energy so that it does not reach Pluto, and therefore Pluto's beams become death beams. The most obvious demonstration of this correspondence would be one wherein Mars, in his aspect of the Bringer of War (Strife), delivers many into the hands of Pluto (Death).

In this mode, Pluto is cold-blooded and can be unflinchingly cruel, and it has been linked with crime (the Underworld). It is the bringer of the cold, hard facts, and the measure of the Last Resort. Thus does Pluto move the masses.

As regards the Arietic positive-regenerative mode of Pluto, however, it is as if the Sun has transmitted Martian energy in Solar-Martian terms so that we get, for example, crime-fighting. It is also Plutonian to fight death, as do surgeons, etc., who work in hospitals.

The positive mode of Pluto, even though co-governing some things which are already given to Mars, still relates not as much to the Arietic fire as to its own coldness, turning against itself and dealing in a cold-blooded manner with that coldness. However, it does resemble the Arien fire in its height of spirituality, which is not attributed to Mars.

Also, as regards birth, it should be noted that this is an occasion when we come into contact with those Plutonian forces which fight death, exemplified in the doctor or mid-wife.

The myth of Pluto and Persephone is qabalistically, i.e., by correspondence, representative of one of the astrological facts we have been considering. Persephone was Spring, which we can instantly associate with Aries. Her arising from the depths of the earth bringing Spring corresponds to the release of Mars-channeled Solar energy emerging from Pluto. Persephone's return to Pluto's domain heralded the submergence of energy, which heralded the coming of winter. (It must be remembered that this is a myth of the Northern Hemisphere.)

Pluto has also been related to sexual activity, where it can represent the extremes, cold-bloodedness, sex without love, the sexual function, per se, as it relates to reproduction, unusually active sex drives, uncommon sexual requirements, etc. It does not rule out love, as in its positive peak of spirituality it can be representative of the greatest love. It must be considered that we all have the Plutonian component in our sexual natures. It is fiercely individualistic, but it is not evil except for the part it plays in cases of rape. This depends upon house and aspects.

Discordant aspects generally show some difficulty in sexual expression, some "hang-up", eccentricity or repression. The good aspects show sexual self-knowledge and ease in sexual expression. Thus Pluto governs the deep innermost psychology of how the native relates to his or her own sexuality. We may attribute the "Free Love" movement to Pluto, which governs changes in sexual mores.

Pluto and Neptune are the two outposts of the Solar System. I include Neptune also because the orbits of Pluto and Neptune apparently cross, and there is a time when Neptune is further from the Sun than Pluto (although it is never as far as is Pluto at its furthest.)

Both planets are representative of the highest spiritual mysteries.

They are like two sentinels at the border of the known world, and thus they govern things unknown. (Note that both Scorpio and Pisces are houses of secrets and the occult.)

These two alone, and Pluto most especially, see and reach what is farthest and deepest. Whichever one is furthest, that one is probably the one most concerned with the new, the approaching, discoveries, etc., and, on the other hand, the one least concerned with mundane affairs.

Pluto, X, the Unknown, our link with the unknown, and the unfolding of the unknown into knowledge, represents the great mystery, and perhaps even the solution of the Mystery. (The perfection of the present system, regarding the Tree of Life, leads me to guess that Pluto really is the last planet in the chain of the Solar System.)

Pluto was discovered in 1930, and I consider this the beginning of what I call the Plutonian Era, the beginnings of which have been aptly characterized by Mr. Benjamine.

The length of this period is indeterminate, since its end would depend upon the discovery of some new and also more distant planet.

(At this writing, 46 years have passed of this era. Since the discovery of Pluto, the planet has transited only the signs Cancer (wherein it was discovered), Leo, Virgo, and now Libra.) We shall shortly make some remarks concerning the planet's future entry into its own negative sign, Scorpio.

Inexorable, often inscrutable, Pluto is a final resolution of the duality into the truth of unity.

Now, with all of what has been said, we might assume nevertheless that Pluto is basically "good" when in Aries and Leo, and basically "evil" when in Scorpio. If this idea has persisted, it must be dispelled. At the point where the mode of Mars becomes the mode of Pluto, there is an overlapping, or a point where the two are alike. Astrologically this dual point of Pluto is worth considering, but if we overlook the fact that Pluto represents the Supreme Unity, we are likely to be misled by the dual considerations.

The influence of Pluto is at its strongest when in Aries, Scorpio and Leo, but in every case Pluto does what must be done. World War II, for example, took place during the early stages of Pluto's sojourn through the sign Leo, its exaltation, a fiery, positive sign.

Pluto may be thought of as the heavenly embodiment of Satan, as in mythology he is Lord of the Underworld, and much can be discovered about the nature of Pluto from such a consideration. But in the final analysis, Pluto is really the Father, seeing to it that "Thy will be done." It represents the power that can both create and even bind Satan, and cast him into the lake of fire.

Now we come to some remarks I should like to make with regard to Pluto's coming sojourn of its own negative sign Scorpio.

It is an omen of especial significance, particularly concerning the 1980's when there will occur a most powerful configuration of planets in Scorpio.

Uranus is presently transiting Scorpio, and we have already seen several major earthquakes. Consider also the interest in disaster films and films exploring the occult as well. (Earthquakes have been related to the fixed signs, of which Scorpio is one, and as the House of Death, I would say it is chief of these in this regard.)

Uranus, here in its exaltation leading the way, signifies an extra added impetus of the Cosmic Will. Considering the coming of Pluto to Scorpio, and the powerful configuration to which we have referred, we can only assume that the cosmic Will is that there be a great paying of karmic debt, i.e., a major cleansing of the earth of its unrighteousness. Unless it is no longer necessary, unless man can quickly and truly learn to love his neighbor as himself, under the coming configurations more and even greater major disasters will occur. We are likely to face, in fact, one of the world's greatest catastrophies.

Remember that Pluto is the planet of the last resort; if there is no option, the last resort will be resorted to. The momentum is building up even now. Major upheavals of the earth are only a portion of the dire probabilities. Other forms of mass death are also probable. Undoubtedly there shall be a greater and deeper turning to God on the part of many.

Consider *Liber AL vel Legis*, a masterwork of Aleister Crowley. Written in Cairo in April of 1904, the book made a statement about the 1940s which is worthy of your attention: "I am the warrior Lord of the Forties."

We can see the accuracy of this prediction.

Now consider that it is further written: "the Eighties cower before me, and are abased."

The reader is advised that he might do well to take some time to explore the Edgar Cayce predictions for the last half of the twentieth century. The famed psychic's predictions include major catastrophes for New York and California. I suggest this only as a possibility.

Revelations and other prophetic books of the Bible will also be found to contain relevant keys.

A spiritual rebirth is a certainty. Whether or not this will require a great cleansing of the earth is in the hands of man. The warning signs will increase. If man does not heed, there will be no alternative, and there can be only one last warning.

This purging, I must advise, does appear inevitable.

Of course, it is also possible that there is a most exalted and fortunate significance attached to this great climax in Scorpio. Who is to say whether this may or may not signify the Second Coming?

Here the astrologer's work becomes like that of the priest and the exorcist, and so I close this chapter with these words:

"This is my commandment, that ye love one
another, as I have loved you." (St. John,
15:12)

LESSON 6

Further Keys Of Astrology.

We have seen that the universe is permeated with order, the Creator's own system of correspondences. (Ultimately, everything is God, or, we might say, a symbol for God.)

We have seen that at the very heart of this system is the Tree of Life composed of the 10 Sephiroth, the primary principles linked with the numbers from one to ten. Everything is regarded as an emanation from the Sephiroth.

Astrology, then, accords with one of the Sephiroth. (The import of this correspondence is the link between Astrology and Uranus, which immediately implies, therefore, that Astrology should be a means of Wisdom (Chokmah).

This sephira governs the Qabalah itself, and Magick, which relies heavily upon the use of correspondences. And as there are links between Astrology and the Qabalah, and Magick and the Qabalah, there are links between Astrology and Magick, the most obvious being Talismanic Magic (i.e., as the Constellatory Art), for which one must know well Astrology.

§ § §

I. We now refer the reader to pp. 15-19 of Aleister Crowley's "Astrology" for several of the truly great keys of the Science.

From this chapter I quote only the following:

> "A glance at the horoscopes of the greatest men of whom we have on record shows that generally speaking the planets form exact or very close aspects and also — this is the important point — that all or very nearly all the planets are interwoven."

II. The next key is something Carter considered worth experimenting with, and it is a method related to the one exployed in Horary Astrology. Personally, I have found this idea of Carter's to be something much more than a worthwhile experiment; it is one of the master keys of Natal Astrology.

This extremely powerful method consists in using the natus as if it were 12 different charts. The natus as we know it, with the proper ascendant, is to be considered as the Key Chart. The entire process of chart delineation is the same up to this point. However, next we use the 2nd House cusp as the ascendant. The new chart, with all its new houses, with its new angularities, etc., becomes the Chart of the Key of the 2nd House Mode. While the Key Chart remains the ultimate guide and check, the 2nd House Chart acts as an enlargement, a further exposition.

Thus the 2nd House is now the ascendant of an entire chart which refers strictly to the 2nd House Mode. The new second house becomes a new clue. The new 3rd House becomes yet a further clue as to how neighbors, relatives, brethren, communications, etc., would affect the 2nd House Mode. We then check the new 4th house, its relationship, noting that planets herein are angular in this regard, etc.

The method proceeds through all of the houses in like manner, and when we are finished we proceed to take the 3rd House as the ascendant, and proceed through the taking of each of the houses as the ascendant.

This is an extended, laborious method, but such corroborations as will be gained make it worthwile.

LESSON 7

An Exposition Of The Methods And Uses Of The Astrological System Given, Employing The Natus Of Aleister Crowley.

The following exploration of the natus of Aleister Crowley has as its purpose only the exposition of this system, and will not venture into the realm of detailed delineation.

Aleister Crowley, the Beast 666, is our subject. His incarnation fulfilled the prophecy contained in the Revelations of St. John the Divine. His unique and awesome place in human history provides an excellent opportunity to demonstrate this system. He was a Magus, but there were factors in his formula which were uniquely his own. His personal magickal attainment is inspiration to the spirit, but we must remember that it is our own Holy Guardian Angel whom we seek, and not Crowley's. His written expositions of the truth, of the mysteries, of magick, of yoga, of the Qabalah, are masterworks, nonetheless. Yet how notorious a being this Aleister Crowley was! (See CHART IX.)

First, let us consider the Ascendant, which is Leo, ruled by the Sun. The number which Crowley took, 666, is a solar number. Leo signifies authority, and Crowley certainly assumed authority! Note that the Sun forms two aspects within the orb of one degree, which gives it power, even though it is cadent. (The two aspects are the sextile of Uranus, and the trine of Saturn) Considering that Uranus and Saturn are angular, we already begin to see the great vigor of the man.

In regarding the Sun's square to Mars, let us note what has been said by Raphael of a cardinal square involving one of the luminaries. It produces fame, or notoriety. (Mars in Capricorn, again, is especially vigorous.)

CHART IX

THE NATUS OF ALEISTER CROWLEY

RISING SIGN ___♌___
RULING PLANET ___☉___
RULER'S HOUSE ___3___
RULER'S SIGN ___♎___
RISING PLANET ___♅___

FIRE ___♅___
WATER ___☽ ☿ ♃___
AIR ___☉ ♀ ♄___
EARTH ___♂ ♆ ♇___

CARDINAL ___☉ ♀ ♂___
FIXED ___☿ ♃ ♄ ♅ ♆ ♇___
MUTABLE ___☽___

ANGULAR ___☿ ♃ ♄ ♅ ♇___
SUCCEDENT ___☽___
CADENT ___☉ ♀ ♂ ♆___

POSITIVE ___4___
NEGATIVE ___6___

OWN SIGN ___♀ ♄___
EXALTED ___♂___
DETRIMENT ___♅ ♆___
FALL ___☉___

BIRTH TIME ___11:30 P.M.___
BIRTH DATE ___10-12-1875___
BIRTH PLACE
___LEAMINGTON SPA___
LAT. ___52° 18' N___
LONG. ___1° 32' W___

GRAND CROSS

7 1°- ORB ASPECTS & 4 PARALLELS

14°♈48' MC

ASC. 6°♌58'

19°♌10'

6°♌58'

IC
14°♎48'

PLANET	☽	☉	☿	♀	♂	♃	♄	♅	♆	♇	ASC.	M.C.	♌	DEC.
☽					✶	⊡				P✶	⊡			4° 9'
☉			P☌	□		△	✶					☍		7° 32'
☿				☌	□	□	☍	☍	P□	⊼				18° 55'
♀					□		△	✶	☍	⊼		☍		8° 32'
♂									△					24° 10'
♃							☍		□			⊼		12° 59'
♄							P☍	□		✶	∠			16° 18'
♅								□	△	⊡				15° 43'
♆									□					10° 28'
♇										∠				4° 24'
ASC.										△				18° 32'
M.C.											☌			5° 52'
♌														

TABLE OF ASPECTS

All that we have considered of the Sun as ruler portrays what may be called a powerful concurrence.

Here it is a concurrence for power, authority, and vigor.

In considering the Sun as Tiphereth (Beauty), let us remember how wisely it was said by the poet that "truth is beauty; beauty, truth." Let us recall that Jesus Christ said, "I am the truth".

The Supreme Beauty is the Presence of God. Crowley was undeniably concerned with the things that are of God. Magick, in fact, may be likened to an aesthetic. Beauty, which implies majesty, also then implies power.

The Sun also represents self-expression. He is Apollo, musician and poet, and therefore given to artistic expression. Herein is yet another facet of beauty, namely, its creation.

The spirit of the muse did exist in Crowley who was, among other things, an outstanding poet. (Venus conjunct the Sun in the 3rd house of writings is an important co-indicator.)

Next we consider Uranus, because it is in the first house. (I consider all first house planets as "rising planets".) This first house key is none other than the planet of Chokmah, of active Wisdom, the Magickal Will, of the qabalah, astrology and the tarot. As we know, Crowley's major contribution to the world are his writings on these subjects. Uranus (Chokmah) corresponds to the grade of Magus, which he attained.

Further Uranian concurrence comes from the angular and dignified Saturn in Aquarius (sign of Uranus,) and also Mars in Exaltation in Capricorn, which comes under Uranus as well as Saturn in this system. (Again, the closest aspect in the chart is Sun sextile Uranus.)

The Sun and Uranus in debilities, coupled with the dignities of Saturn and Mars, suggests Geburah, Severity. Observe the powerful opposition of Saturn to Uranus. The fact of dignified malefics is another clue and key. Again, note that Libra, the sign housing the Sun (also Venus), represents the scales of Justice (Geburah).

The mission of the Beast was not one of mercy but of severity. Witness two examples from that work of his which he apparently considered his most important, "Liber AL vel Legis":

1. "Mercy let be off: damn them who pity!
   Kill and torture, spare not; be upon
   them!"

2. "With my Hawk's head I peck at the eyes
   of Jesus as he hangs upon the cross."

Uranus stands atop the White Pillar of Mercy, it is true, but it houses the malefics with dignity.

The kerubic angular cross formed by Uranus, Pluto, Saturn and Mercury, portrays the work of Crowley as a great challenge; its fixed nature shows also the heights of both pleasure and pain which were to be embraced by the man. But the real key to the chart is not this distracting grand cross, per se, but the opposition between Uranus and Saturn, considered with the Sun, whose position suggests mediation. The aspects formed by these bodies are out-standing in the chart in that they fall within ¼ degree of exactness. Thus, the nature of Crowley is seen as mediated between two modes, Chokmah and Geburah, the grade of Magus and the specific magickal work, i.e., beyond the writings (Sun in 3rd house).

Neptune is the most elevated planet; this again suggests the Pillar of Severity.

I agree with those occultists who claim Crowley made a false step in assuming the grade of Ipsissimus, which corresponds to Kether (Pluto). While Uranus is in its detriment, it is nevertheless the signature planet by virtue of its first house position and force. Pluto's detriment, on the other hand, is not as well counter-balanced, nor is it responsible for any planet's dignity. Pluto is strong, but with the Moon, the Receptive, and with Mars in the house of service and the work. Here we have first a sextile and then a trine. But Pluto squares Uranus and Saturn, and harmonized best in him in his reception as a Magus of his orders from the Crown.

Since we can see the perfection of Uranus rising in Leo, we can also see that it could not be in the 6th house so as to help represent (with the Sun in the 3rd house) writings of a magickal nature. Nevertheless, in this qabalistic system, we have a significant link between Uranus and Capricorn, because it is affirmed as a ruler, albeit the Secondary. Observe how the dual consideration of Capricorn on the 6th cusp elucidates all that we have considered of the Uranian and Saturnian elements in the work.

We have said that Uranus represents the magickal Will. We must not omit making the point that the Word Crowley chose as a Magus, as being the one which captured his entire message, is Thelema, which means Will.

Taking Saturn by herself, observe how perfectly this system is borne out, in that Crowley's Heirophantic task is disclosed by the presence of the planet of Severity in the 7th house, which represents, among other things, one's public.

The Understanding (Neptune) is present in the higher mind (the 9th house), but it is cadent (mental), whereas Saturn is angular.

Jupiter (Mercy) is in the 4th house where it worked for him more than it did through him. Jupiter's only harmonious aspect is its conjunction with Mercury, and, oddly enough, we find that his enlightening writings (Mercury) constitute his significant Mercy.

As Heirophant, however, his Magickal Power was employed in the creation of Ordeals, and we believe that there was tremendous scope to this work, that he thereby affected the very course of history. Thus have we pointed out the emphasis of Geburah, as these ordeals were severe.

(". . . he may make severe the ordeals." - Liber AL.)

Now let us take, for example, the 10th house, and demonstrate how, using this cusp as the ascendant, we can corroborate various details about the career.

Chart X represents the 10th House Key.

Here, Pluto is rising; it still is, of course, referrable to the occult. Uranus rules the new 10th house, as Aquarius is now on the cusp. This is also fitting.

Take Uranus in the 4th house. The angularity concurs with the 4th house angularity of Jupiter and Mercury in the chart proper, and therefore casts further emphasis on the home, with regard to the career. Uranus exemplifies here the magickal environment and its importance. That Uranus is angular in the 4th house of the 10th House Key, tells us there should be an important link between career and home. In the case of a Magus in modern times, this has to be the case.

A magickal house is essential to high magick, as those acquainted with this art will know. Witness the importance of 418

CHART X

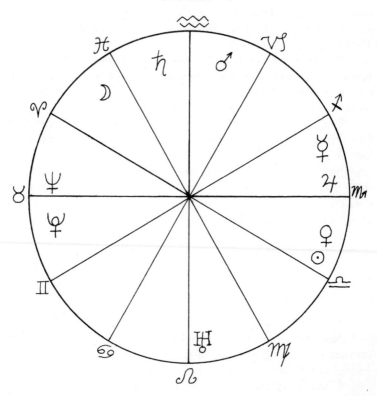

Boleskine to Crowley! The sextile to the Sun and Venus now falls in the 6th house, which is, among other things, the house of ceremonial magick.

Let us consider another point, one in the key chart first (with the true ascendant). Note the harmonious aspect between the 7th house Saturn and the 3rd house Sun. While the marriage of Crowley to Rose Kelly was ill-fated, she exerted a favorable influence relevant to his writings. If we miss this in studying the key chart, we cannot miss it in the 10th house key chart where, in relationship to the work, we find Jupiter in the 7th house, and it is even conjunct Mercury! Those who know the story of Crowley's coming to write Liber AL will know how important a role Rose played in this inspiration.

The 10th house Saturn portrays all that we have said about the work of severity (initiation).

(The reader unacquainted with Crowley, and interested in more information about his life, is advised to read "The Confessions of Aleister Crowley" edited by John Symonds and Kenneth Grant, and published by Bantam Books in paperback.)

PUBLISHER'S NOTE: This book was accepted for publication by Weiser's on September 20, 1976. Since then there have already been several "major upheavals of the earth," as the author predicted.

APPENDIX

BIBLIOGRAPHY-SUGGESTED READING

1. *THE QABALAH OF ALEISTER CROWLEY*, published by Samuel Weiser, Inc.

2. *THE BOOK OF THOTH*, by *THE MASTER THERION* (Aleister Crowley); published by Samuel Weiser, Inc., in paperback.

3. *ASTROLOGY*, by Aleister Crowley; published by Samuel Weiser, Inc.

4. *LIBER AL VEL LEGIS*, by Aleister Crowley; published by Samuel Weiser, Inc., in paperback.

5. *BOOK FOUR*, by Aleister Crowley; published by the Sangreal Foundation, Inc.

6. *THE PRINCIPLES OF ASTROLOGY*, by Charles Carter; published by the Thesophical Publishing House, Ltd., a Quest paperback.

7. *THE ZODIAC AND THE SOUL*, by Charles Carter; published by Theosophical Publishing House, Ltd.

8. *ESSAYS ON THE FOUNDATIONS OF ASTROLOGY*, by Charles Carter; published by Theosophical Publishing House, Ltd.

9. *THE ASTROLOGICAL ASPECTS*, by Charles Carter; published by N. N. Fowler & Co. Ltd.

10. *THE INFLUENCE OF PLUTO*, by Elbert Benjamine; published by The Aries Press.

11. *THE GUIDE TO HOROSCOPE INTERPRETATION*, by Marc Edmund Jones; published by the Theosophical Publishing House, Ltd., a Quest paperback.

12. *TETRABIBLIOS*, by Ptolemy; published by Loeb Classical Library.

13. *THE CONFESSIONS OF ALEISTER CROWLEY*, edited by John Symonds & Kenneth Grant; published by Bantam Books, in paperback.